Zen

Thorsons First Directions

Zen

Martine Batchelor

This book is dedicated to the late Master Kusan and all the people in
Korea who have been a great help and inspiration on this Zen journey

Thorsons
An Imprint of HarperCollinsPublishers
77–85 Fulham Palace Road,
Hammersmith, London W6 8JB

The Thorsons website address is: www.thorsons.com

Published by Thorsons 2001

10 9 8 7 6 5 4 3 2 1

Text derived from *Principles of Zen*, published by Thorsons 1999

Martine Batchelor asserts the moral right to
be identified as the author of this work

Editor: Jillian Stewart
Design: Wheelhouse Creative Ltd.
Production: Melanie Vandevelde
Photography: Henry Allen and PhotoDisc Europe Ltd.

A catalogue record for this book is available from the British Library

ISBN 0 00 711016 2

Printed and bound in Hong Kong

Contents

Zen

Zen is a school of Buddhism that emphasizes th
awakening one's true nature and uncovering one

ractice of meditation as the key to
nate wisdom and compassion

Introduction

Zen has been associated with many different things: Japan, archery, motorcycle maintenance, a certain aesthetic of black and white and pure lines, to name a few. In the past two decades, it has become popular in the West, especially in America. Zen has inspired individuals to simplify their lives or to look at them more creatively. Zen has influenced many artists, writers and poets. It has been used in business practices and even in sport to help competitors hone their minds.

Zen actually means meditation. It comes from the Sanskrit word *Dhyana*, which means meditative state in the Buddhist tradition. This word was transliterated as *Chan* by the Chinese when Buddhism went from India to China. This Chinese character is pronounced *Son* in Korea and *Zen* in Japan.

Zen has many aspects. It has grown within the Buddhist tradition over many centuries in different countries. It has influenced the cultures in which it has developed as well as being deeply influenced and changed by those same cultures. For this reason Zen practice is

slightly different from country to country. However, there is a certain body of texts and principles that are common to all Zen schools: the idea of the Mahayana and the Bodhisattva vows; of Buddha nature and of sudden awakening; all of which I shall explain. Zen is about self-development, about experiential practice which helps you to see life directly and to act with wisdom and compassion. It is something that you do while learning not-doing.

I started to practise Zen when I became a Buddhist nun in South Korea. I studied under various Korean Zen masters, in particular

Master Kusan, who inspired me with his great kindness, lightness and incisive mind. I stayed ten years and it was an opportunity to practise meditation ten hours a day for six months of the year and to live a Zen monastic life in a traditional Buddhist country. The monastery was nestled deep in the mountains covered with pines, azaleas and maples.

It was a simple life with few amenities and a hot bath once every fifteen days. The days followed the sounds of the bells; it was a disciplined life but also a liberating one. Slowly one realized who one truly was and how one was so deeply connected to the whole world. Zen can be very dramatic but also very ordinary. When I left the monastery and joined a Buddhist community as a layperson in England, my second training started: to put into daily practice what I had learned all these years. Zen has to be lived to be true Zen.

* Note on transliteration: Zen names and traditional words are generally written in Chinese ideograms, which are pronounced slightly differently in China, Korea and Japan. Throughout the text, Chinese names or words referring to Chinese Zen will be written with the Chinese pronunciation and the same for Korean and Japanese names and words. Words such as Zen, Rinzai, Soto, Zazen, Koan which are better known in the Japanese pronunciation remain the same throughout the text. C: indicates the Chinese pronunciation, K: indicates the Korean pronunciation, and J: indicates the Japanese pronunciation.

Basic Principles

Mahayana: The Great Vehicle

All Zen schools belong to the Mahayana tradition of Buddhism. Mahayana means 'Great Vehicle'. This Buddhist tradition is known as 'Great' because it contains various different approaches to the spiritual path. The different approaches appeal to different people, thereby allowing as many as possible to be liberated from suffering. Zen is not only for monks and nuns but also for laypeople. Anyone can practise this path and be liberated regardless of status, knowledge or gender.

A Great Vow

One of the characteristics of Mahayana Buddhism is the Bodhisattva ideal. A Bodhisattva is someone who dedicates his or her life to enlightenment and to helping others achieve it for themselves. Bodhisattva means 'Enlightenment Being'. The Bodhisattva practises the six paramitas of generosity, ethics, patience, effort, meditation and wisdom. Paramita (that which has reached the other shore) is generally translated as 'perfection'. By developing and cultivating the six paramitas one is able to reach the other shore of enlightenment.

The Bodhisattva starts on his or her journey by awakening the deep motivation to free all sentient beings from suffering and by taking the Bodhisattva vow, making the firm resolution to attain enlightenment for the sake of all beings. In the Zen tradition, the vow is expressed in a fourfold way. In many Zen ceremonies, the four 'Great Vows' are generally chanted to conclude them. They are also chanted at the beginning of Zen retreats. They are considered the foundation of Zen practice and are the motivation for practice itself.

Sentient beings are numberless, I vow to save them all.
Delusions are inexhaustible, I vow to cut them all.
Dharma gates are limitless, I vow to penetrate them all.
The Buddha's way is unsurpassable, I vow to achieve it.

For a Bodhisattva, the practice is undertaken out of compassion and a great aspiration. In Zen, compassion is linked with wisdom; the two are inseparable. So it is a compassion that comes from a selfless intention but also a wise intention. We are not being kind because we are expecting something for ourselves or because we know what is best for us is best for other people. We act compassionately after listening to the needs of others and also knowing our own limitations.

Generosity is very much a part of this compassion: being generous in mind and heart towards ourself and others, not being kind only to people we like or who are pleasant to us, nor only when we have plenty of time and it suits us. This Zen compassion could be seen as very altruistic and demanding but as one cultivates Zen one realizes it is within us already, and Zen practice helps us to lower the screens and barriers which stop our natural, wise and equanimous compassion from flowing freely.

Buddha-nature

In Buddhism, there are various schools of thought about Buddha-nature. Some traditions see it as a seed to develop in practice over aeons and some see it as a natural state that is covered by our delusions and can be uncovered at any time. Zen belongs to the latter approach. The Zen tradition was very much influenced by the Avatamsaka sutra which states that all sentient beings are Buddhas and all Buddhas are sentient beings.

Buddha is Mind, Mind is Buddha

Zen reacted against the idea that enlightenment and Buddhahood were remote conditions; so far away that one might not even get started, being too discouraged by the lengthy process. Zen is saying, 'Look, here and now! We are alive, we can see, hear, taste, smell, think. We can be a Buddha if we only let ourselves be one.' In peaceful and clear moments, but also when we respond wisely and compassionately in difficult circumstances, we realize that they might be more to us than we think. Zen is not about becoming an idealized perfect person but more about living who we are and can be in our more spacious moments.

From this idea of Buddha-nature being intrinsic came the dilemma: why can't we see it and why should we practise? From these questions arose the debate about sudden and gradual awakening and practice which exists to this day in the Zen tradition. Some Zen schools believe that practice and enlightenment are both sudden, which raises the question: Why does it take even ancient Zen masters at least eight to twelve years for any breakthrough to happen and why do they continue to practise afterwards? Korean Master Chinul's way of looking at this debate seems to resolve those questions. He suggests that enlightenment is sudden, followed by gradual practice which in turn might help to provoke more awakenings followed by more practice.

However, one cannot control awakenings. Nothing is guaranteed. It is very easy to say 'let go!', it is very difficult to do it. In the Zen tradition, awakening is often mentioned, but over and over again, Zen masters will advise us not to be caught by the idea and glamour of it. They often say it is like seeing something for the first time that has been with us all along. It is like a fish looking for water until it realizes it is swimming in it. So this Zen awakening is not metaphysical and will not take us to some other dimension, nor is it going to transform us in a split second into Mother Teresa or some venerable ancient Chinese master. But hopefully it will make us more aware of our own innate wisdom and compassion and help us to live more fully from these two qualities. In Zen, it is said:

Buddha is Mind, Mind is Buddha.

Three Trainings: Ethics, Meditation and Wisdom

Master Kusan used to tell us in his Zen talks that it was essential for all of us as Zen students to train in ethics, meditation and wisdom. These were the basis for any Zen practice. Most importantly they had to be practised in unison. It was like a tripod: with one or two of its legs missing, it could not hold anything and was pretty useless. In the same way, one had to practise the three trainings together for them to be even more effective. A focus on ethics by itself could make one narrow-minded, meditation by itself could make one a little detached and self-absorbed, wisdom by itself could make one a little dry and analytical.

Compassion for Ourselves and Others

Ethics, or morality, are considered important because it has to do with our relationship to the world, people, things and how what we do affects ourselves and others. Zen ethics come out of Buddhist ethics which are based not on rules but on compassion and wisdom, and the notion that as practitioners we intend to dissolve suffering for ourselves and others. In a general way, it answers this question: What would be the most compassionate and wise thing to do? The five basic precepts express this ethic in terms of restraint, of not causing any suffering or more suffering:

do not kill
do not steal
do not have damaging sexual interaction
do not lie
do not take intoxicants

In terms of positive action, the five precepts are encouraging us to be harmless, generous, disciplined, honest and clear-minded. They are intended to be cultivated not only in body but also in mind and speech, not only towards others but towards ourselves. In the Zen tradition, there are also the Bodhisattva precepts, a list of ten major and forty-eight minor precepts that remind us to live with awareness and compassion.

Quietness and Clarity

The second training is meditation. When we meditate, we cultivate concentration and enquiry. Concentration helps to still the mind and enquiry helps to make the mind clearer. In order to still the mind, one concentrates on one object. It can be the words of a question (huatou), the breath, the present moment itself. The aim of the concentration is to stay as long as we can with the meditation object. It is quite difficult as the mind has the tendency to wander to the past, to the future, to the shopping list for dinner tomorrow. We need to remind ourselves of our intention to meditate, to focus on the question or the breath, so we have to come back repeatedly to the object of concentration. After a while we come back more quickly and stay longer on the object. Master Hsuyun said:

A thousand thoughts give us the opportunity to come back to the question a thousand times.

So being distracted is not the problem, staying distracted is!

The effect of concentrating and coming back is threefold. First, our mind is more peaceful because there are fewer thoughts engaging it, since we are concentrating on one thing. Secondly, our thoughts become less agitated and obsessive because we do not feed and indulge in our patterns and habits of mind like ruminating, judging, daydreaming, planning, fabricating, etc, as we come back again and again and cut their threads. Thirdly, we are more aware of ourselves and our surroundings as each time we come back, not only do we come back to the question or the breath but we also come back to the present moment. This has the effect of allowing us to be truly aware, alive and present, experiencing this life, this being.

The other aspect of Zen meditation is cultivating enquiry and brightness of mind. This is done by questioning, looking deeply, staying alert in awareness. It stops the mind becoming dull. The aim of meditation is to cultivate a state of mind which is equally quiet and bright.

Meditation is not only about relaxing the mind but also about the mind being clear and sharp and through that the mind can be used to its fullest potential for understanding and wisdom. Slowly, one learns to see the world in a different way, more open and full of potential.

Potential for Change

The third training is wisdom. Zen wisdom, in simple terms, is knowing to drink out of a cup, that it is a cup and not a bucket, and being fully present in the drinking, the taste of the tea, its colour, its fragrance, with no grasping of the cup, the tea or ourselves or anything else apart from that. It is not about how many books we have read or how much intellectual knowledge we have accumulated. It is about seeing the characteristics of life which in Buddhist terms are impermanence, unsatisfactoriness and emptiness or non-self.

In Zen, impermanence and death are often impressed upon one. But this does not make Zen people gloomy or pessimistic – on the contrary. By experiencing or understanding impermanence deeply we realize the preciousness of life and the potential for change. It is very easy for us to take life and people for granted. We generally believe that we will live for a few more years yet. We think it is other people who die – until it threatens us.

I realized impermanence when I saw the last breath of my father. This changed me irrevocably. I look at my family, myself, my friends in a very different light. I realized how human, how frail we all are. As Master Kusan used to say:

Our life rests upon a single breath.

When you are driving your car very fast to an appointment, is it better to risk dying, or to arrive late? When you have an argument with your partner over the washing up, would you feel differently if you recognized that he or she might die tomorrow?

Recognizing impermanence makes us realize that things can change. We have a tendency to fix, to 'permanentize'. We have a headache, we feel it will last at least a week. We have a problem, we tell ourselves it will last forever and become very anxious. How are we going to stand this terrible thing, day in, day out? It is very rare for anything to last very long, be it our feelings, our thoughts, or even the world around us – everything changes constantly. If we accept that things change, then we open the door to an array of possibilities for ourselves and others.

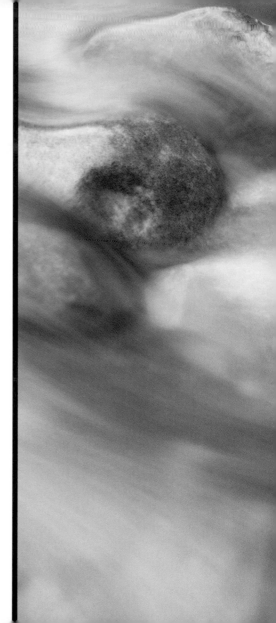

Letting Go

With the wisdom that comes from experiencing impermanence, we realize that lovers, friends, family, possessions, jobs, houses, etc, are only there for a short time and cannot give us lasting happiness; even if we are seduced by the hope that they will. We work very hard to achieve various things. We get a new car or a new job or a new lover. How long is it before frustration appears? Soon we find that the car is not going as fast as we had hoped or we are worried that somebody is going to scratch it. As for the new job, we feel that the atmosphere in the office is not pleasant enough after all, or the job is not as satisfying as we would have hoped. And if only your new partner would wash the dishes or be more romantic, then truly you could have it all and be happy.

It does not mean that we cannot appreciate and care for what we have but nothing can give us total, for ever, lasting happiness because we and they are impermanent and so unsatisfactory in terms of our hope for it. Understanding this will help us to strive less, to appreciate more and to be content with what is. Yunmen said:

Every day is a good day.

Being Enlightened by All Things

The final part of wisdom is understanding emptiness or non-self. Zen is not nihilistic, saying that everything is empty or that we do not exist. It is suggesting that we are not existing independently, separate from anything else and that inside us there is not a solid, unchanging kernel of something that is 'Me'. First, if we look at ourselves, can we say that since we were born there is something within us that has never changed? Imagine being a two-year-old baby, then a thirty-year-old adult, then sixty years old. How many changes in body, mind and speech have happened in these sixty years. Where is this constant, unchanging self?

We are an endless flow of conditions. The conditions are particular and definite because of our specific parents, genes, history, social circumstances. These conditions are unique to us. There is therefore a relative sense of self, but this is not constant nor can it be reduced to one state or thing. We have so many roles (mother, daughter, teacher, friend, customer, etc), so many different feelings and moods (happy, sad, elated, anxious, tired), how could we be just one thing? Even physically, one day we are tired and unwell and we look awful, another day, preparing to go out to a party, we look beautiful and radiant. The idea of non-self does not negate ourselves but actually helps us to discover how multi-faceted we are, how many possibilities we contain, how much there is to discover and uncover.

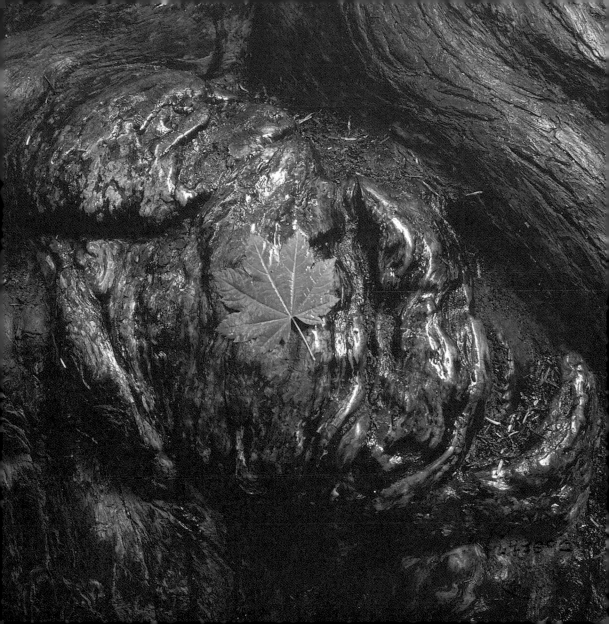

Realizing emptiness is to see that nothing exists separately or independently from anything else and therefore there is nothing to grasp. Again, looking at ourselves, who are we? Why do we feel so separate, so cut off? This is a strange delusion. We are totally interdependent with the whole world. For example, when we breathe, the world is constantly entering through our nostrils, our mouth and our pores into our body. Furthermore, when we are with other people in a room, we are breathing the same air, their out-breath goes into our lungs and vice-versa. How much more intimate can we be!

Other things we depend on are food, clothes and shelter. Without these things we could not survive. So we are dependent on all that supports our life; in turn, these things – food, for example – depend on something else for them to be. Reading this book, you might be sitting on a chair. What is this chair? What makes it a chair? Where is the chairness of the chair, the self of this chair? Is it in the back, in the legs, in the cushioned part? Without any of the parts it is not a chair but any part by itself is not the chair either. It becomes a chair when all the components are put together and we sit on it. When the chair is in

the way, we kick it and think it is a terrible chair. When we are tired, the chair is luxurious and soft and we think it is a wonderful chair. Terrible one minute, wonderful the next – what is the true state of the chair? We do the same with people. We attach qualities to this imaginary, solid self and say: 'Claudia is good, John is bad', and generally 'for ever after' is implied. They might have certain tendencies but it is likely that they will be good or bad according to their own circumstances and our own preferences. The teaching on emptiness is trying to tell us that things and people are not as solid or as separate as we think they are. It is also trying to make us look beyond our simple assumptions and one-sided ideas in order to see a much bigger picture, and finally to grasp less and appreciate more. Dogen, the founder of the Soto (C: Tsaotung) Zen tradition in Japan, expressed this succinctly:

The way of the Buddha
Is to know yourself,
To know yourself
Is to forget yourself,
To forget yourself
is to be enlightened by all things.

Three Attitudes: Great Faith, Great Courage and Great Questioning

Great Faith, Great Courage and Great Questioning are the three qualities one is encouraged to cultivate in Zen practice and all Zen masters have expounded on them.

The Sun is Shining behind the Clouds

Great Faith is faith in our own potential as Buddha, not in something outside of ourselves. Many different reasons might bring us to Zen practice: a friend, a teacher's talk, a book, a search for spirituality, and so on. As we begin to sit, in the quietness and clarity of the meditation, we realize that it is like coming home. There is a certain ease and simplicity. We start to have more faith in ourselves and in our potential.

Great Faith might come upon someone suddenly, but generally it grows with practice. At the beginning, it is more like a belief and we feel rather separate from it. But as we continue, we see some changes in ourselves, we stop grasping so much at details, we open to possibilities, and peace and clarity become more familiar. We see ourselves better, we start to have faith in ourselves and the Zen practice. When suddenly we have some insight like Master Huangpo, we realize that this is not special, just our natural way of being. As he said:

When at last in a single flash, you attain full realization, you will only be realizing the Buddha-nature which has been with you all the time.

However, now our vision is screened so we have to practise, but this practice is sustained by the Great Faith. It is like the sun being covered by thick clouds, we do not see the sun but we know it is there and it will appear again. In the same way, our intrinsic Buddha-nature is covered by delusions and ignorance, but they too come and go. The great faith will sustain us both when our practice goes well and when it does not. So the Great Faith is the basis and the ground for Zen practice.

Great Courage

We need Great Courage to continue on the path Great Faith has taken us upon. For example, Korean Master Hyobong used to sit on a frozen river so the fresh air would keep him awake as he meditated for days and nights. Master Kusan used to sit on the edge of a cliff to keep himself alert when he meditated. I met a Zen nun who had been in silence for ten years to help her be less distracted in her meditation practice. All this requires Great Courage, but nobody told them to do this, they were inspired by Great Faith and determination.

What kind of courage do we require in this modern world with its complexities and urgencies? We need the courage to live in the present and not in the past or in the future. We need the courage to break our habits and patterns of thought. We need to let go of our preferences, impulses and desires. We have such a tendency to be lost in our negative thoughts or our hopeful dreams, or to give in to despondency or laziness. When we do this, we are creating strong habits. How can we change this painful behaviour? We actually need Great Courage to stand firm when we are buffeted by recurring desires, depressive thoughts, negative resentments or beautiful daydreams. We must come back again and again to *this* moment and to the practice of being quiet and clear in awareness.

The following story – about an island inhabited by many monkeys – is often used to demonstrate how our habit patterns limit us. The islanders catch the monkeys by hanging coconuts with sweets inside them. The monkeys, attracted by the sweet smell, put a hand through the hole in the coconut and catch the sweets but cannot get the sweets or their hand out because the hole is too small. If a monkey lets go of the sweets, he can get his hand out and be free, but he wants the sweets, so he holds on and is then captured. It is the same with us: something is enticing so we hold onto it; through the holding we might experience pain but we cannot let go because we want it so much or it seems so attractive. Again we need Great Courage to look beyond the seduction and remember our intention to let go of suffering and to benefit ourselves and others.

Great Questioning, Great Awakening

Great Questioning is traditionally called Great Doubt as in this Zen saying:

Great Doubt, Great Awakening,
Little Doubt, Little Awakening,
No Doubt, No Awakening.

Doubt can mean vacillation in English. In Zen, doubt means questioning. If we want to awaken we need to produce a Great Doubt or Questioning in order to go beyond our usual concerns and anxieties, misconceptions and delusions.

There is a paradox between Great Faith and Great Questioning. We need faith to anchor us and questioning to open us. With faith only, we might stagnate and become narrow-minded, with questioning only we might become disturbed and agitated. These two qualities balance and support each other.

The Buddha strongly emphasized questioning and knowledge born of direct experience. In Zen, we are invited to see life as a question. We are encouraged to open to the 'don't know' mind and to embrace the insecurity of uncertainty. This does not make us confused; on the contrary it allows us to wonder at life like a child and to find marvels in the most ordinary. This is not an intellectual enquiry, we need to be engaged with the whole of our being. It is said that we have to question with the marrow of our bones and the pores of our body. Dogen, asking himself how the Buddha-nature could be represented, thought that the only way it could be expressed was through the question: 'What is this?'

Master Kusan used to say that we needed to question meditation itself. We had to be careful not to grasp at any states, good or bad, and to maintain a balance between quietness and clarity. If we were too quiet we might become dull, so we needed to introduce more enquiry. If we were too focused on enquiry we might become agitated and would then be encouraged to bring more concentration into our meditation. He said we needed to be like hens hatching eggs. The hen moves the eggs at the bottom of the pile – the ones which are cooler – to the top and then moves the top ones down to the bottom so they all have an even temperature. We usually like to know just what to do and then do it, but in this way meditation can become mechanical. Great Enquiry or Great Doubt prevents this and keeps the practice fresh and lively.

In Zen, we are encouraged not to lose our beginner's mind, to be open and to avoid becoming too professional. For example, Master Chaochou, after being a revered master for many years, left his temple to travel on his own as a simple monk. His intention was to continue his training by learning from anyone he met, whether it was a five-year-old child or an illiterate farmer.

History

Zen was developed in China after Buddhism entered that country in the first century CE. Buddhism was a foreign religion brought from India to China by merchants and travelling monks. Over the centuries the Chinese made Buddhism their own and transformed it in various ways. Many different Chinese Buddhist schools arose. The Zen school was the one that survived successfully the tribulations of Chinese history and was transmitted to Korea and Japan. At the root of Zen is Buddhism and the Buddha's life and teachings.

From Buddha to Bodhidharma: A Special Transmission

The Buddha was born in India 2500 years ago. According to the legend, he was born a prince with great riches and lived within the precincts of a vast palace. However, in his late twenties, he left the palace four times to see the world. There he saw a sick person, an old woman, a

dead man and a mendicant. These encounters confronted him with his own mortality and frailness. He realized that suffering was inescapable. He then decided to leave his palace and his wife and young child and become a mendicant to find an answer to the predicament life, old age, sickness and death presented to him.

After six years of adhering to different spiritual practices under various teachers in his search for an answer, he finally sat down alone under a tree (which became known as the *Bodhi* – enlightenment – tree). Six days later, still seated in meditation, at dawn he saw the morning star and awakened. After his awakening to the origin of suffering and its cessation, the Buddha taught for many years. The Buddha's core teaching is that there is suffering. The origin of suffering is craving. The cessation of suffering is attained by eliminating craving and there is an eightfold path which leads to the end of suffering. The eightfold path is right view, right motivation, right speech, right action, right livelihood, right effort, right mindfulness and right concentration.

After the Buddha died, Buddhist monks and nuns spread his message and methods across India and bordering countries. As already stated, Buddhism reached China in the first century CE. There it met already established systems of philosophies and religions: Confucianism and Taoism. The first task was to translate the Buddhist texts into Chinese. Through this endeavour, over many centuries Buddhism became quite scholastic. It is thought that as a reaction to these scholarly tendencies Zen Buddhism arose with an emphasis on meditation and experiential wisdom achieved through direct awakening. An episode of the Buddha's teaching has come to be known as the first Zen story, although it predates the establishment of what is known as Zen.

One day, the Buddha was giving a talk to a great assembly of monks, nuns and laypeople. At one point, he held up a flower, displayed it to the crowd and remained silent. Only Mahakasyapa, one of his monk disciples, understood his meaning and smiled. The Buddha smiled back.

This is considered the first Zen transmission between master and disciple. Twenty-seven other Indian Patriarchs followed until the Indian monk Bodhidharma, who is reputed to have gone to China in 479 to transmit the Buddhist teachings, and around whom many Zen legends have centered. These words, attributed to Bodhidharma, are the most often cited as representing the spirit of Zen.

A special tradition outside the scriptures
No dependence upon words and letters;
Direct pointing at the heart of man,
Seeing into one's own nature, one attains Buddhahood.

Chinese Chan: A Sudden Teaching

After Bodhidharma, Zen transmission went on through a succession of patriarchs, each developing and passing the teaching on to the next. Around 700 CE the teachings branched out and there started to be various lines of transmission, many of which continue to this present day. Each Zen master has a transmission booklet that has been given to them by their teacher when their awakening is recognized and 'sealed'. This process is called receiving 'Inka' (Dharma Seal).

From 700 CE onwards, various schools of Zen arose, of which the Linchi (J: Rinzai), and the Tsaotung (J: Soto), survive to this day. The Linchi School is named after Master Linchi (died 866) who was renowned for his shouts and his hitting style. For example, once he was asked:

'What about the cardinal principle of the Buddha-dharma?'
Master Linchi gave a shout.
The monk bowed low.
'As an opponent in argument this young reverend is rather good,'
the master said.

These Zen shouts are called Katsu. They are used to wake up the

students to their own Buddha-nature instead of being lost in conceptualization or theories, by bringing them back to the experience of this very moment.

From the Linchi School came the tradition of the koans (C: Kung an, K: Kongan) which are test cases used in Zen meditation practice. There are 1700 koans which are compiled mainly in *The Gateless Gate* and *The Blue Cliff Record*. These are records of encounters between Zen masters and their disciples where often the master says something enigmatic that the student has to resolve by questioning without using the intellect. These encounters provoke the student to awaken by stopping the discursive mind and opening to one's own nature.

The Tsaotung School advocated the unity of relative (that which has to do with ordinary life) and absolute (that which has to do with the transcendent or awakened life). This unity was developed through several stages called the 'Five Ranks'. Also known as the 'Five degrees' of enlightenment, each stage takes one closer to the fifth rank where total unity is attained. This led the school to practise 'Silent Illumination', that is 'just sitting' without doing anything. Just sitting – where one tries just to be, to exist and to be fully aware of that – was considered enlightenment itself.

Korean Son: A Syncretic Vision

Buddhism entered Korea in the 4th century CE and in the following centuries five Buddhist doctrinal schools came into being. The Avatamsaka and the Popsong schools were the most influential on the future development of Zen in Korea as they prepared the ground on which Zen would grow. The Avatamsaka School took its name from the *Avatamsaka Sutra*, a Buddhist text which emphasizes the interpenetration of all things and teaches that Buddhas and sentient beings are the same. The Popsong (Dharma-nature) School was founded by Wonhyo, one of the most original thinkers in the history of Korea. His approach was syncretic as he tried to create a sense of unity among the various trends of Buddhist thought at that time.

Zen finally reached Korea around 630, although it took a while to become popular. When it did, the influence of Wonhyo made itself felt. Instead of continuing the conflict with the doctrinal schools, a syncretic approach organically emerged where the practice of Zen was provided with a solid theoretical underpinning. The first teacher to succeed in promoting an effective and enduring syncretic view was Chinul (1158–1210). With Wonhyo, Chinul is considered the most influential figure in the history of Korean Buddhism. To this day, his many texts influence the life and practice in Korean Zen monasteries and nunneries.

In his *Admonitions to Beginning Students*, he writes:

When the master goes up to his seat to preach the dharma, do not be overawed by it and, as before a steep precipice, turn away ... Listen to the sermon with an empty mind; then it will certainly be an occasion for you to attain enlightenment. Do not be like those sophists who have studied rhetoric and judge a person's wisdom only by his eloquence. As it is said, 'A snake drinks water and produces poison; a cow drinks water and produces milk.'

Japanese Zen: The Transmission Continues

In 552, Buddhism was introduced into Japan from Korea. However, there were other schools of Buddhism in Japan which had a much stronger influence on the religious life of the country at that time, so Zen did not rise to prominence until the Kamakura period (1185–1215). Eisai (1141–1215) is considered the founder of the Zen tradition in Japan. He built the first temple of the Rinzai (C: Linchi) sect in Japan, and later became abbot of Kennin-ji, the first monastery in Kyoto where Zen was taught above any other Buddhist teachings. It is here that Dogen met Eisai.

Dogen (1200–1253), the founder of the Soto (C: Tsaotung) Zen tradition in Japan is one of the most important Buddhist figures in that country. Dogen studied in China under Master Juching (1163–1228), a fierce, uncompromising monk who believed that the Great Way was not concerned with inside or outside and that Zen was 'dropping away body and mind', that is: forgetting our body and mind, not being so attached to our ideas, pains and pleasures. He taught zhigandazu (J: Shikantaza) as a form of meditation. As one sat, one did not try to answer any questions or riddles nor try to gain awakening.

Dogen's understanding was confirmed and he received the Dharma Seal from Master Juching. He returned to Japan in 1227, where he wrote many important works that are still followed in temples all over Japan, and founded Eihei-ji, which is still one of the two main monasteries of the Soto Zen school.

Ten Oxherding Pictures

The Ten Oxherding Pictures describe the path to enlightenment and self-development in the Zen tradition. A series of poems and commentaries on the poems are also connected to them. You can see these pictures adorning the walls of Zen temples in China, Korea and Japan. It is the representation in folk images of the training of the mind, body and heart in Zen practice. They depict a young oxherder searching for and taming an ox.

I. Searching For the Ox

In this picture, the young oxherder is in nature looking a little lost, running here and there. He is searching for something but he is not even sure what he is looking for. This represents the stage when we have not started on the spiritual path yet but we feel somewhat uncomfortable and unsatisfied. There are faint stirrings within us. We think that if we had enough material things we would be happy. We would like to have a house with a nice garden or enough money to buy whatever takes our fancy. Perhaps we hoped that a good relationship or a worthwhile or highly-paid job would give us lasting happiness. But nothing seems to completely satisfy us, to bring us that elusive long-lasting happiness. Events keep happening which disturb our dream world. Something seems to be missing. We are like the oxherder in the picture, there is a refreshing stream, beautiful trees, colourful butterflies and wonderful birdsong but still he is not satisfied. Like us, he is anxiously looking for something, inner peace, contentment, clarity.

2. Seeing the Footprints

In this picture, the oxherder finally sees some footprints. It represents the stage when we decide to do something about the dissatisfaction. We look around for something. We discuss philosophy, read about psychology and various states of consciousness. We hear about meditation and Buddhism or Zen. We might have a friend who is practising or we might listen to a talk by a Zen teacher. We are impressed by the peacefulness and clarity of the Zen teacher, we are attracted to the Zen stories but we stop there. We just read about it. It becomes part of our repertoire of ideas but we do not apply its tenets. So, very little changes, we continue to have the same sufferings, the same disturbing emotions and the same negative patterns. Reading or hearing about Zen only is not going to make a great difference in our life.

3. Seeing the Ox

In this picture, the oxherder finally sees the ox half-hidden among the trees. This image represents the stage where finally we decide to really do something. We are not totally sure yet what is the best method and what exactly we need to do. So we try various things. One week we visit a temple, another week we talk with a teacher. We continue to read books to find a good way to practise.

Finally, we might try Zen meditation and as soon as we sit down for a while we experience some peace. We realize that this is something we can do ourselves and it is beneficial. We might also try to cultivate the precepts and be more harmless, generous, disciplined, honest and clear. Again we see the point, we become familiar with the ideas not only at an intellectual level but also at an experiential level. We think that we have found something and we get very excited about it.

4. Catching the Ox

In this picture, the oxherder has finally caught the ox with a rope. But the ox does not want to be caught. The oxherder has to hang on tightly as the ox jumps fiercely and drags him hither and thither. We feel very much like the oxherder when we start to meditate. As soon as we sit down with the aim of concentrating on the question or the breath or just being aware, our mind is flooded with thoughts, memories and plans and our body is not comfortable. We start to have pain in the back, then in the knees, then our cheeks start itching. We try various postures. Like the oxherder we have to be firm and hold on tightly. There are many obstacles: restlessness, sleepiness, daydreaming, etc. We have to realize that for the last twenty, thirty years we have cultivated many habits which promoted distractions and when we meditate we go against all these habits. It is going to take some time before we dissolve the power of these tendencies.

Sometimes meditation goes well and we have to be careful not to be attached to that ease because that too is impermanent – even though as we continue to practise the sense of ease lasts longer and happens more often. Sometimes the practice is difficult: thoughts seem intractable and sleepiness so heavy, but that too passes a little faster as time goes by.

5. Tending the Ox

In this picture, the oxherder is gently tending the ox and the ox is not wild anymore. After having held on tight and sustained the practice for a while, it becomes easier. We are more comfortable with the sitting posture. We can sit still without feeling restless. We are not fighting with our body and mind any more. We are more present and we can concentrate for a certain period of time. We have gained some quietness and clarity which helps us in our daily life.

The oxherder is still holding on to the rope loosely because he knows that although the fight is over, he must remain vigilant. The ox seems subdued but it could jump off at any moment. To practise Zen we have to be confident but aware of not becoming arrogant. We might feel that we know all about Zen but we still need determination and discipline as the powers of distractions are strong. This picture represents a stage of maturation and ripening accompanied by care.

6. Riding the Ox back Home

In this picture, the rope has gone. The oxherder is sitting leisurely on the ox playing the flute. The ox knows where to go without being told. This is an image of ease, leisure and freedom. Some people believe that Zen is very strict and serious or that to be spiritual one has to be gloomy or indifferent. On the contrary, as we advance in the practice we find it is about joy and creativity. As we slowly release the attachment and grasping which used to create so much tension, laughter bubbles within us. We begin to take ourselves less seriously and enjoy life so much more as we open to its changing and ever-fluctuating nature. We dance and sing with life. We have become friends with our body and mind.

This picture also shows us that there is a place for creativity in Zen. As we accept ourselves and the world our potential unfolds, fears and insecurities dissolve and we can express ourselves creatively. It might be through music, painting, poetry, cooking, gardening, being with children or old people. Everything we do can become an art, it is not a duty anymore; it is a way to express our true nature.

7. Forgetting the Ox, the Oxherder rests Alone

The ox has disappeared and the oxherder is resting alone at home. Until now there was this idea that there was something to do, something to practise. There was a separation between ourselves and the practice. There was a dualism between what was spiritual and not spiritual, what was Zen and not Zen. At this stage, we become united with the practice. It does not happen just when we sit on a cushion in a special room. Everything becomes meditation. Awareness becomes as natural as breathing. This is Zen in daily life. We take one thing at a time, fully present to it, and when we move we let it go without residue. We are at peace with ourselves, our mind, body and heart, with the whole world. We do not even need to try, to discipline ourselves, because now the practice and the cultivation of the precepts come unheeded. We do not have to do it, it does itself. As Master Kusan used to say: 'You are one with the question. It is the question that walks, goes to the toilet, looks at the countryside'. Harmlessness and generosity come naturally. In this state, you cannot even think of being unkind or telling lies, those kind of thoughts do not arise.

8. The Ox and the Oxherder are both Forgotten

Now the oxherder and the ox are both gone. There is only a black circle. It represents emptiness. Earlier, when we became united with the practice, there was this idea that it is 'me, I' that was practising. Until now there were strong notions of me, mine. Now this has gone too. We realize that nothing belongs to us truly, we can only care for it while it lasts. We also experience that we do not have a solid, separate identity. We are a flow of conditions. We cannot identify with our feelings, our thoughts, our possessions. They all come and go. They rise upon certain circumstances, stay a while and disappear.

Everything is made up of conditions which are ever-changing. There is nowhere to go, nothing to stick to. We realize that we are more than any of the parts that constitute us. The recognition that we cannot hold onto anything is a great liberation. A great burden is let go of. We feel so light. We realize that everything comes out of emptiness. Only because of emptiness can things change and flow. Emptiness is not a vacuum, a black hole, but the possibility of endless transformations. There is no more grasping, or self-created barriers and limitations. The Buddha-nature can shine through and express itself fully.

9. Returning to the Original Place

In this picture, there is water flowing, flowers are blooming and birds are singing. The practice does not stop at emptiness. If we attach ourselves to emptiness it could lead to separation and isolation. So we have to go one stage further, re-entering the world where 'having forgotten ourselves, we are enlightened by all things'. We realize the interdependence which is at the root of all life. When we are having breakfast in the morning, as we eat and chew a piece of toast we connect with the grain, the green shoots, the earth, the sun, the rain, and appreciate the efforts of all the people who made that piece of toast possible.

   Our life is ordinary and just as it is but we look at it differently. We realize that everything expresses the truth of life and awareness, and is talking to us. We do not skip on the surface of things any more but we are intimately related and experiencing every single item without grasping or rejecting. We are not locked in on ourselves anymore but fully open to the world. We are not frightened but on the contrary exhilarated. The world is us and we are the world. All this practice – just to realize what was on our very doorsteps!

10. Entering the Market Place with Helping Hands

The final picture shows a ragged, pot-bellied man walking barefoot bearing a sack full of goodies. This last stage represents freedom, wisdom and compassion. We are not encumbered by appearances. We adapt freely to high and low places. We find spirituality everywhere, it is not confined to monasteries and secluded places. Meditation and realization do not make us passive but active. We are deeply connected to the world, we feel its suffering and we want to respond and help. Our bag is full of joy, compassion, understanding, loving-kindness, wisdom and skilful means.

We naturally give to ourselves and others what is beneficial. We listen deeply, we observe unobtrusively and respond appropriately. When we give we do not expect anything. We are not superior to others when we help them, on the contrary helping them is like helping ourselves and we are grateful they give us that opportunity to extend ourselves. When we love it is with total acceptance. We do not help only people we like but also people who are difficult. However, we do not force our ideas – our opinions, what works for us – on others. We try to bring lightness into people's lives. We do not take it all too seriously.

When we look at the Ten Oxherding Pictures we have to be careful not to think that self-development and Zen practice go in a straight line. It is more like a spiral. We go round and up, hopefully. We go back to different stages but with more understanding. We deepen our realization of each stage as we continue on the path. We still have delusions and attachments to shed. We discover more ways to develop concentration and enquiry further. Master Kusan had three different major awakenings, and each time he continued to practise even more. The last time, his own teacher, Master Hyobong, said: 'Until now you have been following me; now it is I who should follow you.'

Zen
Meditation
Exercises

At the heart of Zen practice is meditation. By 'turning the light back onto oneself' in meditation it is possible to see one's own true nature and in so doing become awakened. The Buddha taught four postures to meditate in: sitting, walking, standing and lying down. In formal Zen meditation, sitting and walking are specially used.

Sitting like a Mountain

Sitting meditation is an art. In Zen practice, one might sit for long periods of time repeatedly. Great emphasis is laid on maintaining a good posture so the sitting is comfortable. Such a posture will help the mind to be clearer and the breathing to be smoother and healthier.

We can sit in different postures. Traditionally these are the full lotus posture and the half-lotus posture. In A *Generally Recommended Mode of Sitting Meditation*, Dogen wrote:

Spread a thick sitting mat where you usually sit, and use a cushion on top of this. You may sit in the full-lotus posture, or in the half-lotus posture. For the full-lotus posture (see page 58), *first place the right foot on the left thigh, then the left foot on the right thigh. For the half-lotus posture* (see page 58), *just place the left foot on the right thigh. Wear loose clothing and keep it orderly. Next place the right hand on the left leg, and the left hand on the right hand, with palms facing upward. The two thumbs face each other and hold each other up. Now sit upright with your body straight. Do not lean to the left or tilt to the right, bend forward or lean backward. Align the ears with the shoulders, and the nose with the navel. The tongue should rest on the upper*

palate, the teeth and lips should be closed. The eyes should always be
open. The breathing should pass subtly through the nose. Once the
physical form is in order, exhale fully through the mouth once, sway left
and right, then settle into sitting perfectly still.

Nowadays people also sit in quarter-lotus with the foot on the opposite calf, or in the Burmese style, or kneel on a cushion, or on a bench. One can also sit on a chair if one finds it difficult to sit on the floor. In the Burmese style (*see page* 59), the left foot is not put on the right thigh but just in front of the right leg. Kneeling on a cushion (*see page* 59), the legs are placed either side of the cushion; sometimes several cushions are used for that position. Kneeling on a bench (*see page* 60), the legs are tucked under the bench; one might use a soft pad on the bench in order not to cut the circulation to the legs. Sitting in a chair (*see page* 60), one sits with the back erect, half-way on the seat, trying not to lean against the back of the chair. One might put a cushion on the chair or a cushion under the feet. If one sits fully in a chair, with one's back touching the back of the chair, one must be very careful not to slouch and get into an unhealthy posture which would constrict the breathing and be harmful to the body.

1 Full-lotus

Right foot on left thigh,
left foot on right thigh.

2 Half-lotus

Left foot on right thigh.

3 Burmese style

Left foot against right lower leg on floor.

4 Kneeling on a cushion

Legs on floor either side of cushion.

5 Kneeling on a bench
Legs tucked under bench.

6 Sitting on a chair
Half-way on the seat if possible.

In all these postures, the traditional Zen way is to have the eyes half-closed to prevent drowsiness or agitation. The eyes are not fixed on anything but just gazing downwards at a forty-five degree angle. The back is straight but not rigidly so. The shoulders are comfortably low and the head rests lightly on the shoulders. The chin should be slightly drawn in. When sitting on the floor we are trying to form a triangle with the legs as the base and the head at the top so that we feel stable and grounded but relaxed at the same time.

The hands are on each other, palm up as instructed by Dogen and the thumbs are lightly touching each other. The hands are in front of the navel, the arms slightly apart from the body, and sometimes it helps to place a small towel or a thin cushion on the legs on which the hands can more easily rest.

We breathe quietly through the nose. We do not control the breathing but let it flow naturally. We try not to breathe noisily. Often it is recommended to breathe with the lower abdomen. It is suggested that it helps to make the breathing deeper. In this system, when one inhales the lower abdomen fills up, when one exhales it becomes concave; one also needs to be able to relax the diaphragm.

When sitting in half-lotus or the Burmese posture one does not need to always put the same leg on top or in the front. One can alternate the position of the right leg and the left leg. Generally, one sits on two cushions in the lotus, half-lotus or Burmese style: a rectangular flat pad or cushion (J: Zabuton) to make it more comfortable for the legs and a round cushion (J: Zafu) to get the right height for the bottom. Sometimes one might put some smaller cushions under the knees so one is more stable if both knees cannot rest on the Zabuton. In the kneeling postures one only uses the flat cushion (Zabuton).

Walking with Awareness

As well as sitting meditation (Zazen), Zen involves walking meditation (J: Kinhin). There are various styles and speeds. In China, one walks clockwise around the Buddha statue in the meditation hall or outside in a circle, slowly, or at a steady pace, or fast with the arms hanging alongside loosely. In Korea one walks inside the meditation hall anti-clockwise but on the outer rim of the cushions at an ordinary pace with the arms relaxed and loose. In China and Japan, the cushions are situated closer to the walls and in Korea they are laid in two lines more towards the middle of the room.

   In Japan, the walking is very formal and organized. You put the thumb of the left hand in the middle of the palm and make a fist around it. You place this fist in front of the chest. You cover the fist with your right hand. The elbows are kept away from the body and form a straight

line with the forearms. In some places you may be told to turn the fist downward and rest the other hand on it. In other places you will be advised to place one hand on the other and just hold them to the chest. You are supposed to start walking with the right foot, then you advance by taking only half a step for each breath in and out. You are walking slowly and smoothly as if you were standing in one place.

Whatever the form of the walking meditation, one continues practising what one has been doing in the sitting posture: counting the breath, being aware or asking a question.

Counting the Breath

Counting the breath is used mainly in Japan and in China in the Soto tradition. You count the breaths from one to ten. When you reach ten, you return to one and start counting again. If you lose count, you come back to one again. Sometimes you might count further than ten, again you come back to one and start again. You can count exhalations and inhalations separately or together.

After you have learnt to be concentrated by counting the breaths, you may be told to move on to just watching the breath without counting. There are two methods. The first one is to observe the breath just as it is without modifying it in any way. You just observe the breath coming in through the nostrils, moving down to the lungs and coming out again. The second method is to observe the breath while consciously modifying it. Generally this is associated with Tantien (J: Tanden), breathing with the lower abdomen. You try to breathe in all the way to the abdomen, then you might hold the breath very slightly for one or two seconds and then let it out again.

In the breath meditation, the breath becomes the object of concentration. Whenever you are distracted you try to come back as soon as possible to the breath. When counting the breath you realize quickly how distracted you can be. It is often difficult to count all the way to ten without thinking of something else.

When first watching or counting the breath it might feel somewhat artificial and mechanical, because in paying attention to the breath you feel you are controlling it more. You need to relax and be confident, then you will become naturally attuned to the breath and become one with it. The question, 'who does it?' will no longer be important. In the end, the breath does itself.

Just Sitting

In the Chinese Tsaotung tradition it is called 'Silent Illumination'. We sit quietly in a good sitting posture and are aware of the whole world and the whole of ourself in this moment. And the quiet brightness of the mind appears naturally as we remain still with no object of concentration but the sitting itself. Master Sheng Yen advises:

You must be at a stage where there is no problem becoming settled, when you can sit with unbroken concentration, with almost no outside thoughts ... [Otherwise] It is hard to tell whether your mind is 'bright and open' or just blank. You can be idling, having very subtle thoughts, and believe you are practising Silent Illumination. You can be silent without illuminating anything.

In silent illumination, there is a gradual stilling of the mind and thoughts slowly become less powerful and more intermittent. They become as light as bubbles, and as insubstantial as froth as the brightness of the mind shines more fully.

   In the Japanese tradition, Dogen refers to the notion of Shikantaza, 'just sitting'. As Yasutani Roshi presents it:

Shikantaza is a practice in which the mind is intensely involved in just sitting ... The correct temper of mind therefore becomes doubly important. In Shikantaza, the mind must be unhurried yet at the same time firmly planted or massively composed, like Mount Fuji let us say.

But it must also be alert, stretched, like a taut bowstring. So Shikantaza is a heightened state of concentrated awareness wherein one is neither tense nor hurried, and certainly never slack.

Shikantaza requires intense concentration. Often it is recommended not to do Shikantaza for more than thirty minutes at a time, as it is difficult for the body and the mind to keep up such a level of energy. Then one can do walking meditation for a little while and start again refreshed. At the beginning one might feel somewhat tense doing this practice, but after a while one can relax and rest in awareness without undue strain.

What is This?

In Korea one generally practises the koan 'What is this?'. 'What is this?' comes from an encounter between the Sixth Patriarch Huineng and a young monk who became one of his foremost disciples, Huaijang.

Huaijang entered the room and bowed to Huineng. Huineng asked: 'Where do you come from?'
'I came from Mount Sung', replied Huaijang.
'What is this and how did it get here?' demanded Huineng.
Huaijang could not answer and remained speechless. He practised for many years until he understood. He went to see Huineng to tell him about his breakthrough.
Huineng asked: 'What is this?'
Huaijang replied: 'To say it is like something is not the point. But still it can be cultivated.'

The whole story is considered the koan and the question itself 'What is this?' the hwadu (C: huatou). One sits in meditation and asks again and again 'What is this? What is this?' What is it that moves, thinks, speaks? Even more before we think, move, speak, what is this? We are not asking about external objects: what is the carpet, the cup of tea, the sound of the bird? We turn the light back onto ourselves: what is this in this moment?

We have to be very careful, this is not an intellectual enquiry. We are not speculating with our mind. We are trying to become one with the question. The most important part of the question is not the meaning of the words themselves but the question mark. We are asking unconditionally 'What is this?' without looking for an answer, without expecting an answer. We are questioning for its own sake.

We are trying to develop a sensation of openness, of wonderment. As we throw out the question 'What is this?', we are opening ourselves to the mysterious nature of this moment. We are letting go of our need for knowledge and security. There is no place where we can rest. Our body and mind become a question.

There are several ways to ask the question. At the beginning especially we can connect the question with the breath. We breathe in, then as we breathe out, we ask 'What is this?'. Otherwise we can try to make the questioning like a circle, we ask gently but steadily, as soon as one 'What is this?' stops another 'What is this?' starts. Once our concentration is firmer, we can just ask the question from time to time and stay with the sensation of questioning it evokes. As soon as the sensation of questioning dissipates we raise the question again, using the words vividly.

Mu

In Japan one generally starts the study of koans by investigating the koan 'Mu!'. When Master Chaochou was asked if a dog had Buddha-nature, he said: 'Wu!'. This 'Wu!' is pronounced 'Mu' in Korean and Japanese. Some people take this 'Mu' as just an exclamation and when practising do not translate it. So the practice is to repeat inwardly the word 'Mu'. This is often associated with breathing from below the abdomen (tanden breathing). One tries to locate the Mu in the abdomen and become one with it.

Others translate the word 'Wu!' as 'nothing', 'without', 'no'. Then one is perplexed by this answer of Chaochou. The Buddha said that all beings have the Buddha-nature. So why did Chaochou say no? What did he mean by it? What was his state of mind before he said it? Then the practice becomes the enquiry of 'What is Mu?'. One continuously asks about Mu. One is perplexed by this Mu, one does not understand it, one does not know. Mu becomes a barrier that one has to pierce through. One cannot let it rest. Mu becomes like a mosquito trying to pierce our skin, infuriating. Yasutani Roshi said:

Don't let go of Mu even for a moment while sitting, standing, walking, eating, working ... To become lax even for a second is to separate yourself from Mu. Even when you go to bed continue to absorb yourself in Mu and when you awaken, awaken with your mind focused on Mu. At every moment your entire attention must be concentrated on penetrating Mu ... You will become enlightened only after you have poured the whole force of your being into oneness with Mu ... Once you realize Mu, you know that nothing can be opposed to it, since everything is Mu ... In the intense asking, 'What is Mu?' you bring the reasoning mind to an impasse, void of every thought ... Trying to answer 'What is Mu?' rationally is like trying to smash your fist through an iron wall ... Only through unthinking absorption in Mu can you achieve oneness ... Mu is beyond meaning and no meaning.

In this kind of enquiry, one has to be careful not to try to figure out Mu with the intellect. This is not an exam test in which there is one specific answer to a specific question. One is trying to experience Mu, not to think it. One is endeavouring to release the fixed mind with its set answers and definitions and open oneself to the world of experience which is flowing, spacious and in flux. After realizing Mu, a Zen student is said to have entered the 'world of Mu'. After this, one trains with various other koans, and Mu continues to be experienced and understood in deeper ways.

On a Retreat

In the West generally Zen retreats are organized for a week at a time. They are, in the main, held in silence. There are some variations in the schedule and tasks according to the teacher, the style, the school, the cultural background.

The Chinese Way

A Chan retreat is quite an undertaking as it is about self-confrontation and challenges one's habits and comforts. One rises at four in the morning and goes to bed at ten at night. The day consists of sitting and walking periods accompanied by two sessions for work, such as cleaning, washing-up, cooking, chopping wood, depending on what is deemed necessary. The sitting sessions last a half-hour but participants may miss the exercise break and continue until the next one if they wish and have the capacity to do so. When there are a few minutes to rest one is encouraged to do voluntary meditation or meditative walking. One can also continue to sit late into the night.

The main rules of the retreat are silence, punctuality and tidiness.

There are three main reasons for cultivating silence on a seven-day retreat. The first one is that it helps the mind to become calmer. As the input and output of words and conversation are severely diminished, there are fewer distractions for the mind.

The second reason is to help us to accept ourselves and become friends with who we are. By being silent for seven days, we get to know ourselves intimately. We learn to appreciate ourselves and our inner potential. In the silence things become clearer and we realize the misconceptions and misapprehensions we can have about ourselves. We become friends with the ordinary human being who is alive, who breathes moment to moment, who longs for peace and clarity.

The third reason is to be with a group of people, to communicate and share with them in a different way. Although we do not speak to each other, we support each other by our mere presence and willingness to be there. No one is better than the next person, we are experiencing the same difficulties. By all sitting together with discipline and sincerity we are helping each other's practice and intention. Master Sheng Yen teaches that the purpose of a Chan retreat is to:

1   *Realize one is not in control of one's own mind.*
2   *Discover how to train the mind in awareness.*
3   *Calm the mind.*
4   *Provide opportunities for repentance and hence regain purity.*
5   *Practise with an individually suitable method that will yield insight.*

Various methods are taught during a Chan retreat from watching and counting the breath to huatou practice and Silent Illumination. Between sittings (Zazen) there is yoga, or slow and fast walking. The walking is in a circle either inside or outside. Every morning and evening there is some chanting and repetition of mantras. For example, the *Heart Sutra*, which is a text about emptiness, is recited twice a day.

There are also talks given by the teacher. They can be formal commentaries on passages from ancient Zen texts or more practical instructions about the practice and the state of mind one is trying to develop. There are also private interviews with the teacher about one's personal practice.

A Modern Korean Retreat

Certain Western meditation teachers adapt the Asian way of practising meditation to make it easier for Western students to attend. Normally in Korea one would get up at three in the morning and sit for fifty minutes at a time and walk for ten minutes ten to twelve times a day until nine or ten at night. This can be very difficult, especially if one is not used to sitting cross-legged on the floor.

During this retreat, as one is walking, sitting, standing, lying down, working, one tries to ask repeatedly and with great perplexity 'What is this?'. The times are not marked with the sound of a bell but with the clap of a 'Jukpi', a thin strip of wood cut in half, two-thirds of the way down. The 'Jukpi' is also used for the formal bowing.

There are three formal bows in the early morning and in the evening. Only people who are comfortable with Zen ceremonies need attend. The three bows can be seen as paying respect to the three Jewels of the

Buddha, Dharma and Sangha, or it can be seen as paying respect to one's own Buddha nature and reminding oneself that awakening is a possibility for everyone.

There is an instruction period in the morning which deals with the technical aspects of meditation, such as the various postures and the different obstacles one encounters. Evening talks present the philosophy and the principles of the Zen tradition in a modern context. At the end of the talk, there is a question and answer session. There are also private interviews, which are generally held in the afternoon, as the meditation and walking session is in progress. The interviews help the teacher to get to know the retreatants and answer any personal questions they might have about Zen or life in general.

A Japanese Retreat

On a Japanese-style retreat, the teacher might teach either the Rinzai or the Soto approach or both depending on the lineage they belong to. People are encouraged to wear black or dark-coloured loose clothes. If one becomes a disciple of the teacher and a follower of that specific group, one might wear Japanese-style Zen garb when on retreat: special loose black trousers or a wide black skirt and a black tunic or a special sitting robe.

Japanese Zen retreats are very formal with many directives on how to behave: how to eat the formal meal, how to enter and leave the Zen Hall, how to sit and walk. For example, one enters the Zen Hall (Zendo) with the hands in the *shashu* position (formal walking meditation posture as described previously), stepping forward with the left foot on the left side of the door.

A bell is rung to indicate the beginning and ending of the meditation period. During sitting meditation periods a person who walks around the room holding a stick will hit you on the shoulder to help ease tension in the shoulders, or sometimes if you slouch or nod, look sleepy or sluggish. In certain centres it is automatic; in other centres you are only hit if you request it.

The retreats are held in total silence and generally eye contact between the retreatants is not recommended. An important part of a Japanese Zen retreat is to go for interviews (dokusan) with the teacher several times during the week or even during one day. The teacher might ask about the koan one is working on, or provoke one to an intuitive response about one's understanding, or discuss the difficulties one might be having. Many students look forward to these interviews and see them as a way to test themselves and their practice.

The talks given on a Japanese retreat are generally carried out in a traditional way by taking a Zen text and commenting on it. The teacher might describe a koan from

The Gateless Gate, explain the various commentaries that were added to it throughout the centuries and make its teaching relevant to the particular retreat. The teacher will also conduct some ceremonies throughout the day similar to those on a Chan retreat, with the addition of the homage to the lineage. This is specific to a Japanese retreat and involves the group intoning the name of each master in the lineage, while bowing at each name.

These Zen retreats are quite intense and are supposed to help us go beyond our small concerns, difficulties and attachments by pushing us beyond our limits.

Obstacles

There are many difficulties one might encounter as one goes on a Zen retreat, especially at the beginning. The first obstacle we are challenged by is pain. It is not only the physical pain of sitting in one posture for thirty minutes or so cross-legged, but also the mental pain of being still for a certain period of time. One is not used to this. The physical pain improves over time. One can also do some stretching exercises like yoga to help limbs become more supple.

It is important to remember that everyone is different in mind and in body. It might be easy for someone to sit in full-lotus and difficult for someone else to sit in the Burmese position even with many cushions. One of the rules should be that if the pain disappears as soon as one stands up and walks then it is negligible. However, if the pain in the knees or ankles continues for some time one needs to find a different posture and combination of cushions and stool or otherwise just use a chair. Some teachers insist on traditional zazen in half-lotus at least, some think it is more important for the mind to be concentrated on the question than to spend most of our time worrying about the pain. It is important to notice that the way we feel about any pain can depend very much on what is going on with our mind. If we are totally engrossed in daydreams, we do not feel any twinges. If we are concentrated, we feel relaxed and solid in the posture.

Sleepiness

Another obstacle is sleepiness or dullness of mind. As soon as we sit down we feel heavy and listless and start to nod. There, two things need to be considered. Did we work very hard before we came to the retreat? Are our body and mind excessively tired? Or is it that we feel fit and awake in other activities but when we sit we become very sleepy, yet as soon as the bell rings the end of the sitting we feel wide awake again. Then sleepiness arises out of escapism, not wanting to deal with ourselves and the intensity of the practice.

There are various remedies to this problem. The first one is to remind ourselves of our intention: why did we come to this retreat? What inspired us to make that decision? Intention is a strong part of what will give impetus to our practice. The other thing we need to do is to observe our posture: as soon as we slouch, our mind will become dull. This is one of the reasons why so much emphasis is put on having a good posture in Zen. A straight, relaxed back will keep us fresh and alert. We might simply need to open our eyes wide for a few minutes to bring more light into our consciousness.

Busy Body, Busy Mind

Another obstacle is restlessness in the body and in the mind. First we feel we cannot sit still, we have pain in the knee, we have an itch in the lower back, we move this way and that way, and things only improve for a few minutes. It is very important then to just sit still and relax into the posture and not give in to impatience. We need to rest in the moment, in the meditation and stop fighting.

When we begin to sit in meditation we realize with horror that our mind seems never to be still. It is running here and there to this memory, that plan, images, worries, dreams, grievances, desires. We may notice a tendency to daydream. This generally starts with the words: 'if I had ...', 'if I was ...'. We may ruminate over some hurt or pain we have suffered in the past, or we may have a tendency to plan. As we are the actor, director, screenwriter and producer of our thoughts we can make our imagined reality extremely pleasant. Alternatively, we judge fairly constantly: are we sitting well or not, is the teacher speaking well or not, is the person sitting next to you bowing properly. On a silent retreat it is easy to fabricate stories out of nothing or very little. The teacher or another retreatant seems to look at you funny. You wonder what is wrong with you and spin a great story about that. We have many such tendencies that we start to see more clearly as we meditate and as we concentrate we start to dissolve the power of these habits over our mind.

Expectations

The higher the expectations we have of what a retreat will do for us, the less likely it is to happen. It is important to be inspired in order to achieve something. However, the more set the goal and the time to achieve it, the more pressure we will put on ourselves. Zen is about openness, not-knowing, questioning, looking freshly at the world and ourselves. We cannot fix and solidify what is unpredictable. We need to let go of our desires even towards awakening and special experiences. What will happen will happen; just be sincere, determined and open.

   Sometimes we might experience special states when we meditate intensely. We might feel ourselves dissolving. We might be without any grasping for a few minutes, totally at one with the question or 'Mu!'. We might experience bliss or a total open heart and love. We have to be careful not to grasp at these experiences and want to replicate them exactly again and again. They come, they nourish us, they show us that we can be different from what we generally think we are. By grasping at them and fixing them we stop ourselves from opening to even better experiences that we might never have dreamt about.

   We also have to be careful when we leave the retreat not to grasp at that either. Your daily life situation is very different from the circumstances of a retreat. We can continue to meditate daily but in a way which fits our circumstances, a little at a time throughout the day whenever there is a gap and nothing is happening. It is useful to continue to meditate formally for ten to thirty minutes a day as regularly as we can manage with our schedule and family. It can also help to join a sitting group once a week or every month to give us support, so we do not feel alone in our Zen journey.

Zen Centres

There are many different Zen centres. Some are well-established monasteries where a traditional Zen lifestyle is lived and practised. Some operate only when Zen retreats are conducted. Some do not have a building as such but meet regularly in various public or private places. What follows is a partial listing, in alphabetical order.

Great Britain

The Buddhist Society offers Zen classes throughout the year.
Contact: 58 Eccleston Square, London SW1V 1PH. Telephone: 020 7834 5858

Community of Interbeing organizes evenings and days of mindfulness, retreats and other opportunities to practise together with others.
Contact: Val Philpott, 12 The Mount, Thornton le Dale, Pickering, North Yorks YO18 7TF.
Telephone: 01751 477246

Gaia House is a retreat centre which holds Zen retreats, week-long and weekend, once or twice a year.
Contact: Gaia House, West Ogwell, Newton Abbott, Devon TQ12 6EN.
Telephone: 01626 333613

Harrow Zazenkai holds regular sittings and occasional introductory workshops.
Contact: 8a Butler Avenue, Harrow, Middlesex HA1 4EH.
Telephone: 020 8422 9356

International Zen Association United Kingdom has various sitting groups throughout Great Britain and Ireland.

They also organize Zen retreats regularly.
Contact: 91–93 Gloucester Road,
Bishopton, Bristol, Greater Bristol,
BS7 8AT. Telephone: 0117 942 4347

Kanzeon Sangha UK organizes a
programme of Zen retreats. There are also
various associated sitting groups around
the country.
Contact: George Robertson, Top Cottage,
Parsonage Farm West, Uffculme, Devon
EX15 3DR.
Telephone: 01884 841026

Throssel Hole Buddhist Abbey is a
training monastery and retreat centre.
People are welcome to visit for retreats
or to join in the life of the Zen
contemplatives. Various Buddhist
festivals are celebrated throughout the
year and Buddhist ceremonies (funerals,
memorials, etc) are conducted for
individuals.
Contact: Throssel Hole Abbey, Carrshield,
Hexham, Northumberland NE47 8AL.
Telephone: 01434 345204

The Reading Buddhist Priory
(176 Cressingham Road, Reading,
Berkshire RG2 7LW. Telephone: 0118 986
0750) and **The Telford Buddhist Priory**

(49 the Rock, Ketley, Telford TF3 5BH.
Telephone: 01952 615 574) are affiliated
centres. There are also associated
meditation groups around the country.

Western Ch'an Fellowship organizes
retreats in a farm, Maenllwyd, in Wales
and weekends in Bristol. There are many
groups associated with the Western Ch'an
Fellowship around the country.
Contact: Simon Child, 24 Woodgate
Avenue, Bury, Lancs BL9 7RU.
Telephone: 0161 7611945

White Plum Sangha organize regular
sittings and Zen retreats.
Contact: David Scott, 21a Aigburth Drive,
Liverpool L17 4JQ.
Telephone: 0151 728 7829

USA

Cambridge Buddhist Association offers
regular sittings and retreats throughout
the year. Contact: 75 Sparks Street,
Cambridge MA 02138.
Telephone: 617 4918857

Ch'an Meditation Center – Institute of
Chung-Hwa Buddhist Culture organize

day-long, weekend and week retreats.
Contact: 90–56 Corona Avenue, Elmhurst,
Queens, New York NY 11373.
Telephone: 718 5926593

Community of Mindful Living
organize retreats, publish and distribute
books, tapes and a newsletter *The
Mindfulness Bell*.
Contact: PO Box 7355, Berkeley, CA
94707. Telephone: 510 5273751

Diamond Sangha/Kokoan Zendo offer
daily sittings, classes, interviews, work,
celebrations and rituals. They also
produce a newsletter *Blind Donkey*.
Contact: 2119 Kaloa Way, Honolulu
HI 96822. Telephone: 808 9460666

**Kanzeon Zen Center of Utah –
Hosshinji** is a residential centre with
morning and evening zazen, introductory
courses, week-long retreats and a
three-month winter intensive Zen
training.
Contact: 1274 East South Temple,
Salt Lake City, UT 84102.
Telephone: 801 3288414

Mount Baldy Zen Center follows a
strict monastic training. The centre is
open all year round and provides various
methods of practice each season.
Contact: PO Box 429, Mount Baldy
CA 91759.
Telephone: 909 9856410

**Providence Zen Center – Diamond Hill
Zen Monastery** offers daily meditation,
chanting and bowing practices. There are
retreats throughout the year of various
lengths and a special three-month retreat
in winter.
Contact: 99 Pond Road, Cumberland RI
02864-2726. Telephone: 401 6581464

Rochester Zen Center offers daily
meditation, various retreats, a residential
training programme and introductory
workshops. They produce a quarterly
journal *Zen Bow*.
Contact: 7 Arnold Park, Rochester NY
14607. Telephone: 716 4739180

San Francisco Zen Center offers various
daily sittings, lectures, courses and retreats.
Contact: 300 Page Street, CA 94102.
Telephone: 415 8633136. It also has a
monastery *Tassajara Zen Mountain Center*
and a farming centre *Green Gulch Farm*,
which have been very influential in the
Zen life of America.

Shasta Abbey offers retreats and Zen training throughout the year.
Contact: 3612 Summit Drive,
Mount Shasta, CA 96067.
Telephone: 916 9264208

Springwater Center offers meditations and regular retreats, conducted in a looser style than the traditional Zen Japanese way.
Contact: 7179, Springwater, NY 14560.
Telephone: 716 6692141

Zen Center of Los Angeles offers daily meditation, retreats, courses and seminars. They also have a Zen Mountain Center which provides winter and summer ninety-day intensives, extended Zen training, and yoga, tai chi, chigong, and environmental retreats.
Contact: 923 South Normandie Avenue,
Los Angeles, CA 90006-1301.
Telephone: 213 3872351

Zen Center of San Diego,
2085 Primrose Drive, Willits, CA 95490.
Telephone: 707 4593771
This centre was founded in 1983 by Charlotte Joko Beck who also created her own independent school, Ordinary Mind Zen School. Retreats and sittings are organized regularly. There are affiliated centres in California and Illinois.

Zen Community of New York,
21 Park Avenue, Yonkers, NY 10703.
Telephone: 914 3769000
The Zen Community of New York is part of the White Plum Sangha. It is directed by Tetsugen Glassman Roshi who was one of the first disciples of Maezumi Roshi to receive transmission. He developed a programme to help the people in the neighbourhood. There is the Greyston Bakery and now the Greyston Family Inn, a centre for the homeless. In 1996, the Zen Peacemaker Order was also created. There are daily sittings and private interviews, Street retreats and Bearing Witness retreats in New York and abroad.

Further Reading

The Blue Cliff Record, Thomas Cleary (tr), Shambhala 1977.

Chan and Zen Teaching, (First Series), Lu K'uan Yu (Charles Luk), Century 1960.

Catching a Feather on a Fan, John Crook, Element 1991.

Cultivating the Empty Field: the Silent Illumination of Zen Master Hongzhi, Taigen Daniel Leighton (tr) with Yi Wu, North Point Press 1991.

Diamond Sutra and the Sutra of Huineng, AF Price and Wong Mou Lam (tr), Shambala 1969.

Guide du Zen, Eric Rommeluere, Livre de Poche 1997 (in French, a very thorough guide to Zen centres all over the world).

A History of Zen Buddhism, Heinrich Dumoulin SJ, Beacon Press 1969.

Minding Mind, Thomas Cleary (tr) Shambhala 1995.

Moon in a Dewdrop: Writings of Zen Master Dogen, Tanahashi Kazuaki (ed), Element Books 1988.

The Shambhala Dictionary of Buddhism and Zen, Shambhala 1991.

The Three Pillars of Zen, Kapleau Roshi, Anchor Books 1989.

Tracing back the Radiance, Robert E. Buswell Jr (tr), University of Hawaii Press 1991.

Zen Flesh, Zen Bones, Paul Reps, Penguin 1971.

Zen Keys: A Guide to Zen Practice, Thich Nhat Hanh, Thorsons 1995.

The Zen Koan, Isshu Miura and Ruth Fuller Sasaki, Harcourt Brace Jovanovitch 1965.

Zen Mind, Beginners' Mind, Shunryu Suzuki, Weatherhill 1973.